Joseph V. O'Connor

**Hints on Preaching**

Joseph V. O'Connor

**Hints on Preaching**

ISBN/EAN: 9783337000141

Printed in Europe, USA, Canada, Australia, Japan

Cover: Foto ©Lupo / pixelio.de

More available books at **www.hansebooks.com**

# HINTS

## ON

# PREACHING

BY

REV. JOSEPH V. O'CONNOR

---

PHILADELPHIA
PORTER & COATES
1894

# APPROBATION:

Rev. Jos. V. O'Connor.

*Rev. and Dear Sir:*—I have read your *brochure*, "Hints on Preaching," and think them excellent, because calculated to make preachers more natural in their delivery.

What Talleyrand said to a young author, "that in his book there were many things new, and many things good, but the good things were not new, and the new things were not good," I can reverse in relation to your "Hints on Preaching."

Yours sincerely in Christ,

✝ P. J. Ryan, *Archbishop.*

Philadelphia, *July 7, 1894.*

# PREFACE.

THIS little book was written at the request of several Priests, who claim to have derived benefit from some hints which I gave them in conversations on the subject of sacred eloquence, and the delivery of sermons.

If only one of my dear *confrères* in the sacred ministry finds help from this book, in the arduous work of preaching, that, for me, will be a sufficient reason for its existence. Or, if I can personally be of service to any Priest who wishes to practise the principles laid down in the book, he has only to command me. No slight reward is promised even to those who only indirectly help the "laborers in the gospel" (Philip. 4: 3).

Every Catholic sermon is good, because it is true. We need, chiefly, to study delivery.

J. V. O'C.

# HINTS ON PREACHING.

## CHAPTER I.

### THE FUNDAMENTAL LAW OF VOCAL DELIVERY.

THE importance of delivery, or, as it is called by the classical rhetoricians, the pronunciation of a discourse, is recognized in all treatises on oratory. Whilst nothing can supply the want of thought, its proper vocal communication is essentially necessary to the great end of public speaking, the persuasion, or, at least, the convincing of the hearer.

It is a common experience to be present at admirable sermons, which are completely ruined in the delivery. The preacher rises for the purpose of being understood. If he cannot, by his voice, make his words intelligible to his hearers, he fails to attain the end which he sets before him, and he may as well remain silent. As perspicuity is the prime requisite of written composition, intelligibility is the first condition of effective preaching. There is a natural pleasure in listening to a speaker, whose words come clear and distinct to our ears, even if he utters nothing but commonplaces. The chief beauty of style, according to Herbert Spencer, is a transparent clearness, which enables us to see, without effort, the writer's meaning. Every expenditure of mental force wearies, and tends to exhaust the brain. If I must struggle to understand the meaning of your words, I come less vigorous to the apprehension of your thought. So, if a hearer must crane his neck over a pew, to catch a word here and there, he will quickly relax into inattention, and finally into a doze.

The essential condition of all intelligible preaching, is articulation. By this is meant the perfect formation of the word, as it falls from the lips. To do this takes time. Sound travels at a fixed rate. Give each word its proper form and time, and wait until it is fairly launched into the air-sea, as the Germans call the atmosphere. If you throw a pebble into a lake, it will form wavelets that go gradually to the bank. This is analogous to the air-waves which sound sets in motion. Do not jumble them together.

Books on elocution are filled with dry tables of the sounds of letters. But the very best way of forming a good articulation is by the whisper. In order to make a man hear your whisper, you must produce all the vocal elements perfectly. When we try to understand a man whispering to us across a room, we observe his mouth, because the shape helps us to know what words he is forming, just as deaf people acquire an amazing facility in understanding our words, from the motion of our lips.

You will be surprised to discover that you can easily make yourself understood in a whisper, at a distance of a hundred feet, provided you articulate every syllable properly. Try this exercise daily, with a companion. The result will be the sensible conclusion, that if you can be heard in a whisper, at a hundred feet, there is no necessity for bellowing, or splitting the ears of your audience.

As the vowel is heard of itself, give all your attention to the consonant. This is the backbone, the joint, or *articulus* of the word or the syllable. All effective speaking depends upon the percussion of the consonant. To swell the voice on the vowel results in mouthing. The clear-cut enunciation of the consonant sends the word like a pistol-shot.

Time, in delivery, is measured, not on the word, but between the words. Send out the first word, clear, articulate, firm. Then pause. Do not drawl the word. You may wait as long as you please, after the word, but not on it. Make your pauses between the words. It seems strange to say, that you cannot be too slow in delivery. Yet such is the rule. The reason is, that your natural impetuosity will hurry you along, in spite of your determination to go slowly. Rein yourself in. Force yourself to speak in a measured tone. Even in the torrent, tempest, and whirlwind of your passion, you must acquire this temperance, this slowness, not of the word, but of the pause.

Good articulation will secure you the advantage of being heard and understood. This is a beauty of speech, for which nothing can compensate. The most eloquent language, the most appropriate gesture will fail of effect, if your words are unintelligible.

Spare no pains to acquire this essential condition. Read aloud a page daily, in a slow, deliberate manner. Get somebody, if it is only the sexton, to go with you into the church, and station him in the last pew. Take your natural conversational key, which is somewhere in the middle register, neither high nor low, and read or speak a few sentences, perfectly articulated. You can also practice the whisper exercise. Within a short time, you will almost unconsciously have formed the habit of speaking distinctly, slowly, and naturally.

Once this habit is acquired, you will rest easy on the score of being heard. You will not be obliged to peer anxiously at the people around the door of the church, to see whether the last man looks as if he heard you. He may have the same kind of face as Lord Thurlow's, of whom Curran said he wondered whether a man could be as wise as Thurlow looked. You will *know* that your words reach every part of the building. An ordinary voice, properly articulated and measured, easily fills a circumference of eight hundred feet diameter, and this, too, in the open air. Test the range of your voice, in an open field, by measuring off four hundred feet, at which point, station a friend, and speak to him in a natural tone, observing a medium pause after each word or two, and not modulating much. You will never be called to speak under greater difficulties; and if you find, as you will, that your words reach this point clearly and distinctly, you need not worry about not being heard in any church or hall. If you are not heard, the fault will not be yours.

Do not proceed a single step in the application of the hints that you will find in this book, until you have mastered the principle of articulation. This is the basis of all elocution. With it, any discourse is tolerable. Without it, the highest oratory is unmeaning jargon, so far as it is addressed to the ear.

The last word of a sentence gives unpractised speakers trouble to manage. Some speakers meet the difficulty, by not dropping the voice at all. This is contrary to a law of speech, which generally marks the close of a thought, by a fall of the voice. This last word may be all important. If the hearer loses it, he loses your thought. A good way to make the last word carry, is to emphasize it a little. The natural effect of emphasis is to raise the voice. If this slight stress is made, the word will carry.

Another, and, perhaps, better plan is to pause slightly before the last word. This requires a new impetus of breath, which carries the word to its destination.

Watch this last word. People will tell you they hear every word except the last. Either stress it, or pause before it. Even if you emphasize it rather forcibly and explosively, this is better than to let it be lost.

If you are annoyed by an echo in the church, use just sufficient voice to be heard. The more boisterous you are, the noisier will the echo become.

In fine, there is scarcely a difficulty in making yourself understood, which cannot be overcome by perfect articulation. It is the fundamental law of delivery.

Leave to young misses the dread of opening the mouth. Form the word well forward in the mouth, and enounce it with due force. Labor hard to overcome a tendency to mumbling, or chewing your words. Recall stuttering Demosthenes, and pluck up courage.

For a priest, the simple reflection should suffice that at least a portion of his congregation derive almost all their knowledge of doctrine and morals, from the pulpit. Unhappily, about the only religious book an American reads, is his vest-pocket prayer-book, and even this he wishes smaller. But he yields to none in his intelligent and respectful attention to a sermon.

# CHAPTER II.

## THE NATURAL MANNER.

EVERY man has his own way of expressing himself. It may be good or bad, but it is his own. Is there any criterion of excellence, any standard of taste in public speaking, as there admittedly is in literary composition? If there is such a criterion, we are bound to observe it.

Can we formulate any rules, by the observance of which, any speaker can hold the ear of his audience?

Broadly speaking, he is an orator who carries his point, the interesting or the convincing of his hearers. He may shriek or splutter his thoughts and arguments, but if he succeeds in persuading his hearers, he has attained the end of speaking. The man with the facts and reasons may disregard every law, but the one of intelligibility, and carry the audience with him, and who shall deny him the orator's crown? The rapt stillness of an audience is oftener a higher tribute to oratorical power, than a storm of shouts. Pure intellectual power, without a single grace of delivery, has won enduring oratorical fame.

But man is made up largely of sensitive faculties. All his knowledge comes to him through the senses. These the orator directly addresses. He speaks to eye and ear. The instruments which he uses partake of material elements. His voice is a sound; his words, vocalized breath. His sphere lies partly in the material and sensible. He must adapt himself to his environment. This determines his methods, and, largely, his success.

Wendell Phillips said that O'Connell's physical presence was half the battle. So was Daniel Webster's. Some have, from nature, a clear, full, resonant voice. Still, let no student despair of attaining some excellence in public speaking, if he labors under no irremediable vocal defect. Horace, who distinguishes the poet from the orator, declares that mediocrity in the poet is insufferable. But there are degrees of excellence in oratory; and it is in the power of any man who can talk, to learn to talk well.

The basis of all art is nature. Pope says "true art is nature to advantage dressed." The verdict of approval is given by the pleased attention of a miscellaneous audience, which no speaking can permanently interest, that is not natural and intelligible. We have only to find out what pleases them, to get a hint of how to proceed.

The natural pose is the most graceful. It consists in keeping the hips well back, the chest raised, the head up, the weight of the body on the balls or forepart of the feet, the heels resting lightly on the ground, the hands falling naturally and easily on the sides. The hardest thing to do on the rostrum is to do nothing. The easy, unconstrained position on the altar or in the pulpit must be studied, until all awkwardness vanishes, and you seem to the manner born.

We learn in childhood to modulate the voice, by the imitation of the sounds of the language we constantly hear. It is true that there are certain tones of the voice, as there are certain gestures, which are natural to mankind, and which manifest themselves in all human speech. But we learn the inflections of our mother tongue in infancy, on the street, at school. A foreigner is instantly detected by his inflection of our native tongue, though he may speak it more correctly than ourselves. If you can modulate all the tones of your native language, in accordance with universal use, you can become a pleasing speaker.

If, from any cause, your intonations and inflections are entirely different from those everywhere heard and uttered around you, you will never attain eminence as a speaker, though you may win attention as a logician, theologian, or scholar. You must use the tones and inflections of the people, if you are to please them. Here, the educated and the illiterate are one. A man may talk bad grammar, and pronounce incorrectly. But his inflections are as accurate as a college professor's. This music of the language, ringing in our ears from infancy, must be heard in the orator's speech, or he will not move the popular heart.

The best way of getting rid of all false intonations, wrong inflections, affected emphasis, and other positive faults of modulation, is to come back to the prevailing tones of common conversation, such as you hear them at table, on the street, in the cars, in general society, from educated and uneducated alike.

In your exercise on this natural manner, you <u>must</u> translate your sermon into the simplest forms of speech, and tell it to your friend or teacher, as you would tell a trifling incident of the day.

In fact, you must exaggerate in private this familiar style of preaching, in order to master the simple conversational tones as applied to grave subjects. We never make a mistake in time, emphasis, force, modulation, or inflection, when we talk to one another at table, or on a walk. When you doubt about the proper way of preaching a sentence, make up something like it, on an indifferent subject, and watch how you say the latter. Depend upon it, that is the right tone. The two sentences: "The Church to-day celebrates the Feast of All Saints," and "There goes John Smith down the street," are pronounced with the same inflection.

You will be timid at first, about adopting

this natural manner. It seems below the dignity of the pulpit. You have so long accustomed yourself to a plaintive whine, a pathetic tremolo, or a ponderous monotone, that you are startled to hear the natural tones of your own voice in the pulpit. You are afraid that the people will look up with surprise at this irreverent innovation.

To prepare yourself for the imaginary ordeal, practise this easy style for a while in private. Give it at least a trial before the bar of your own judgment. Declare relentless war upon all tones, however musical, which you know and feel are not appropriate to the natural expression of the sentiment.

Have the courage for once to talk right straight to the people. Cast all fear to the winds. You are a man speaking to one individual, as if in the confessional, in your room, on his deathbed. Let your congregation be merged into this one poor sinner, whom you are endeavoring to move, to change, to convert to God. He is your friend, your brother, your child. You and he are alone. Speak, as you would then speak, and the profound attention of your auditory will show you that you have struck the right chord.

It is the blending of your own individual manner with this general intonation, or common way of inflecting the language, that will keep you free from imitating others. All imitation is destructive of the best effects of speaking, which must be your own and come from your heart, and be instinct with your own individuality. Be yourself at your best. Have a judicious friend to point out to you your false tones, your pulpit reverberations, your long-drawn-out oh's and ah's. The nearer you approach the natural manner of every-day expression, the better will you preach. Simplicity is the last word of art, as it is the first.

Practice and steady adherence to the natural expression, in the face of inartistic criticism, will give you courage and confidence.

Charles James Fox became the incomparable Parliamentary debater he was, by saying a few words on every bill before the House. He said that he spoke every night he attended the Commons, except one, and he regretted that he did not speak then You must avail yourself of occasions to address your people. You will find a good opportunity of exercising the natural manner, when addressing children. Here you must talk plainly and simply. You must introduce the anecdote, which is nothing, if not naturally told. You will gradually abandon the heavy, monotonous tones which you may fancy are so impressive, and adopt that charming, easy, persuasive conversational directness, which constitutes the perfection of delivery; for, being natural, it lends itself to the highest oratorical flights, which it saves from being bombastic. Where once you thought terrific force was necessary to emphasis, you will now perceive that profound feeling expresses itself with subdued intensity. You will come to understand the poet's dictum : " One touch of nature makes the whole world kin."

# CHAPTER III.

## CULTIVATION OF THE VOICE.

IT is related of Malibran, a famous *prima donna*, that her singing-master kept her a whole year, running the scales. She thought that the second year would introduce her to the study of grand opera, but the master kept her at the same primary lessons. At the close of the year, he said to her: "Go, you are the first singer in Europe."

In cultivating the speaking voice, you have only to use it intelligently, that is to say, naturally, and with ease and comfort to yourself. Never mind the elaborate exercises set down in books of elocution. Shout, sing, declaim anything that pleases you, keep the voice in use, and you will improve it indefinitely.

The chords and muscles used in voice-production grow strong, just as the muscles of a blacksmith's arm, by proper use and exercise. There is only one rule. Keep within your natural range of voice. Avoid the falsetto. Speak neither too high, nor too low. But speak often. Keep at it. If you like to sing, no practice is better. Read aloud. Declaim. Give this practice at least ten minutes a day, if no more.

A deep, strong voice is desirable on many accounts. You can lower your voice several tones, by practising assiduously the intonation of open vowel sounds. Take this line from Tennyson:

"All day long, the noise of battle rolled."

Speak it on your lowest natural note. Repeat it frequently. Roll out the o's and a's, prolonging as deep a tone as you naturally have, and you will deepen and strengthen the voice wonderfully. But keep at it.

The orotund is an acquired voice. Its basis, of course, is nature; but you must practise the low tones, and the open vowels, very steadily, if you desire to obtain it. Keep at the o's. Open wide the mouth, depress the tongue, and say O as long as you can.

The reason why your voice is husky and muffled on Sunday morning, is because you have not used it during the week. Throw open the window of your mouth daily, and let the fresh air down your throat and lungs. Roar, bellow, shout, if you are reasonably secure against arrest, or detention in a crazy-house. Try to make yourself heard above the rattle of ice-carts and trolley cars. Do anything to keep the voice in fair use. This is the only rule.

A celebrated tragedian, who found himself "blown" after a passionate speech, watched an actor who could declaim any length of time, without apparent fatigue. He found the secret—the art of voluntary breathing. Take deep, full breaths, great inhalations that fill lungs, abdomen, and all the organs of respiration. This is the way to keep the bellows full. You speak, just as the organ plays. The apparatus of the human voice is similar to that of any reed instrument. Keep the bellows full, by deep breathing.

See how many figures you can count with moderate slowness, after one full breath, not from throat or chest alone, but from the abdomen. If twenty, this will give you a "pointer" to take breath after the same number of words.

We breathe properly, when we are asleep or quiet. But speaking requires plenty of breath, and we are forced to keep up the supply. Sometimes in our ardor, we forget to take breath, at the proper place, and we find ourselves gasping. Or, we snap a mouthful of air, with our throat or upper chest. Watch the bellows, that is, the abdomen. Breathe deeply from that region, and your voice will continue full and strong.

The happy result of intoning the open vowels o and Italian a, on your lowest note, will be the formation of the excellent habit of speaking from the chest. You will be delighted to find that you can speak for an hour in this way, without any distress or fatigue. But if you speak from the throat—using what musicians call the head-voice—your voice will become hoarse and squeaky, and you will be extremely fatigued even after a fifteen minutes' speech.

Strike that note in your voice, the middle one, from which you easily rise or fall. Keep to that. If you want to speak louder, do not raise your voice, but increase its volume or power, on the same note.

Beware of any note or key which tires

you. It is nature's signal that you are wrong. Get back to the tone that comes easiest and most flexible. Power is always attended with ease. If you feel that you are pulling against the stream, drop the oars, or pull in another direction. A change of key in speaking is pleasant. You can make it with greater ease and less observation than a singer, who must use considerable art, to cover up the slightest fall from concert-pitch. Strike boldly into the familiar conversational tone, if your ear tells you that your voice is becoming strident or husky.

Whatever improves the general health acts favorably upon the quality of the voice. Exercise with the dumb-bells, Indian clubs and general gymnastic of the arms tend to expand the chest. Speaking while going up hill is also a good exercise. Observe the proper attitude in walking and sitting. Do not muffle the throat with scarfs or comforters, unless after the sermon, when you must go out into the cold air.

The full, pure, resonant voice comes from cultivating the lower register. If you have a nasal tone, get rid of it by practising on the lower register. Perseverance will result in the happiest effects.

Why does preaching weary and exhaust you? Why do you dread the physical effort? Believe me, it is because you do not use your voice properly. We can talk for hours without fatigue, and frequently as loudly as we speak, or need to speak, in the pulpit. But we talk naturally. We make use of the natural inflections, the proper pauses, the right cadences.

No sooner do we open our mouth in the pulpit, than all is changed. A dreary monotone strains the vocal chords, just as constant drumming on one key of the piano injures its general tone. Instead of speaking from the chest, we pipe from the throat.

If only for your physical comfort, and out of regard for your health, I implore you to give these hints a trial. Take your time. Inhale full breaths. Speak in your natural, conversational tone. Vary your inflections in accordance with the sentiment. Forget that you are preaching; and soon you will ascend the pulpit, with an elastic step and joyful feeling. Far from fatiguing your body and soul, preaching will become an exercise beneficial to the throat and lungs.

These rules and exercises may seem mechanical; but the vocal apparatus is a mechanism. There is only one way of expressing sentiment with absolute fidelity, and that is, to feel it. But this depends so much on mental and emotional qualities, that we cannot be taught it. "Eloquence," said one of its masters, Daniel Webster, "must exist in the man, in the subject, and in the occasion."

A few hints, however, will set you on a

fair way to succeed in good expression. "What I *know*," said Socrates, " that I can express."

If you comprehend the full meaning, weight, and purport of every sentence that you utter, you will speak it better naturally, than if you applied to its delivery all the rules of all the rhetoricians. The mechanical reading of little children comes from their ignorance of the meaning of words. Your own sermon, really and truly your own, thought out of your mind and heart, will come from your mouth, laden with significance, emphasis, and power.

Study to form each sentence, until it is the very image of your thought. Reflect upon your ideas, meditate them, probe the meaning of important words, and then speak, and you will see what I mean.

Julius Cæsar and Napoleon could dictate to seven secretaries, a different letter, almost simultaneously. But most of us find it hard enough to fix our mind on one thing at a time. If we preach a memorized discourse, we must work with divided energy, unless a perfect committal to memory leaves every other faculty free.

Endeavor to memorize, without specific words, the ideas in their order and sequence. Practice will bring command of language. Never will you reach the full measure of the orator's power, until you are able to do this. One thing at a time is the law for the generality of minds.

When you are possessed with your subject; when it is part of your mental structure; when you have not only brought it forth, but nourished it in the recesses of your heart; then rise to give it forth. You will be surprised at the ease and fluency with which you will speak. It is the divine saying illustrated: "Out of the abundance of the heart, the mouth speaketh."

## CHAPTER IV.

### THE STYLE OF A SERMON.

SERMON is made to be heard, not to be read. That was a shrewd preacher who was urged to print his sermons, and who answered: "Yes, if you print me with them."

I desire to impress upon you this truth, that you have your own way of saying things, and that for you, it is the best. I am addressing educated men, many of whom know more about the theory of sermonizing than I do; but I claim a wide experience in the practice of preaching, and I am deeply convinced, that most of us are on the wrong track, in the composition of our discourses.

My idea of a sermon, is that it is an animated conversation with one person—an ideal person, if you choose—in the audience. In this view, a sermon is not a theological disquisition, an ornate essay, or a Ciceronian oration. You may make use of all that rhetoric teaches regarding the composition of such discourses, but a sermon is none of them. I go so far as to say, that you can preach an excellent sermon that will not read well, or look well in print.

Sit down at your desk, or, better, go out for a walk, and ask yourself: What do I want to say to my people? What truth do I wish to expound? What duty to enforce? What warning to give?

Let your subject lie in your mind. There is such a psychological fact as unconscious cerebration. Your subject will actually grow up in your mind, and the least tending will help it to reach maturity. Talk the matter over with yourself. Be your own hearer. What impresses you, depend upon it, will impress the people. "Where did you get your wonderful knowledge of human nature?" was asked of Massillon. "From my own heart," was his answer.

I may give your vanity a twinge, when I counsel you to eschew originality. We are in possession of the Truth, in full measure, overflowing, heaped into our bosom. We do not need the topics of Aristotle, or the laborious processes of rhetorical invention. *Prædica verbum.* The word is already in our mouth. It is for us only to give it forth.

The final cause determines the means. You must prepare your sermon, from the standpoint of your people's needs. This truth, so obvious, is the one which we continually ignore.

The first thing a lawyer does is to study his jury. Let us take a lesson from him.

Ruskin's rules, not to waste pains on stupid pupils, but give all care to the bright ones, may do for a school of art, but it will not do for a congregation. You do not neglect your bright, intelligent members, (who will admire you all the more) when you adapt your discourse to the understanding of the simple-minded and the illiterate.

You know the range of common language. You hear it daily, in the confessional, from your servants, from that ubiquitous person, the average man. That is the language which I want you to use, purified from slang, bad grammar, and faulty pronunciation.

Be a philosopher. You want these people to receive your ideas. Present them in the only medium in which they can receive them. Be on this point a rigid utilitarian.

Long, rounded periods, classical allusions, closely-reasoned points, perfect syllogisms, abstruse theological terminology are lost on miscellaneous assemblies.

When an army comes to a bridge, the order of "break step" is given. The bridge would give way under the steady, regular, footfalls. The common mind breaks down under a serried column of syllogisms.

You now see the purport of this chapter, and, indeed, of the entire book. As the system of elocution herein defended may be termed the natural and conversational, so the style of sermon advocated, is the simple, obvious, and familiar.

You must learn to talk to the people, in the language of the people, and awaken in their minds the ideas of religion that lie dormant there. To become a successful preacher, you need only tell the people what they already know, but you must tell it to them forcibly.

If you would learn a salutary lesson, ask even a fairly intelligent man, to tell you what he remembers of your last sermon, or of any sermon. Your experience will lead you to this most important conclusion: About one half of a congregation can take home one idea, out of a long discourse. Now you have a clear conception of the limits of your work. You know what you can do. You can drive home one idea, into at least one half of your congregation. This fact must determine your whole composition. It must be, mainly, the amplification of one leading thought, and that within the comprehension of the average man.

Fix that one idea in your head. Resolve to get it into the heads of your hearers. Have no childish fears of repetition. All's well that ends well. Bring every resource to bear upon the elucidation of that one thought. Throw every argument into a figure of speech, an illustration, an anecdote. Draw pictures. Go into word-painting. Remember that the intellects you address are untrained, are little above the grade of childhood. Clothe your logic in flowers. Keep to particulars. The common mind cannot generalize. Your sermon may break every stiff canon of pedantic rhetoric, yet be a glorious success. You are bound to convey one truth anyhow. Make sure of that. Go back to it by another way, and show it again and again. Amplify. Heap up illustrations. They never weary the people, though your severely classic taste may rebel against them.

The art of writing is specifically distinct from the art of speaking. We forget this, and wonder why our well-written sermons fail to make an impression; and our badly-jointed, impromptu talks to the people rivet their attention. Rhetoric discountenances what oratory allows. Oratory delights in fulness, in repetition, in loosely-woven sentences, in exclamations, in parentheses. It follows spontaneously the natural order of thoughts and feelings. The writer must condense, must keep the strict construction, the syntactical collocation. The orator makes his meaning clear, with a wave of his hand, by an inflection of his voice. A pause, an exclamation, a flash of the eye, say all. Speech is only one of his media of communication. You may hardly be able to parse some of his sentences; but his meaning is as clear as the noon-tide. Said Desdemona to Othello:

> "I understand a fury in your words,
> But not the words."

To acquire the conversational style, you must begin by discarding the cut-and-dried formulas of divisions, sections, sub-sections, a, b, c, d, etc. Having thought out your discourse, sit down, and write as simply and clearly as you can. Follow the current of your thought, and do not pause to pick out fine words. Do not write more than five pages of foolscap. If you follow the directions for slow delivery, these will take you about a half-hour, counting the reading of the Gospel, and the announcements. No sermon, except on a special occasion, should exceed a half hour in length.

Practise daily a short extemporaneous address to your table and chairs. These must be your first audience. The advantage of writing is, that it forces you to say your say. The same happy effect follows upon your attempt to speak aloud. We are brimful of ideas, in our own mind. The trouble begins, when we try to express them, to give them a local habitation and a name. Never mind a break-down. You will learn more from your failures, than from your successes.

It would be foolish to decry the advantages of our training in rhetorical composition. But, remember, that "all the rhetorician's rules but teach him how to use his tools." Get clear ideas about your subject. Write them out in plain English. Deliver them, as I have tried to show you, and sit down, when you have said them.

We talk in short sentences. We do not labor to connect them with the elegant junctures, which constitute so high a grace, in an accomplished writer. The orator can afford to neglect these niceties. This will lessen your labor of composition.

If the axiom of Cicero is true, *caput artis decere*, appropriateness is the perfection of art, I hope to have shown that the best sermon is something like that which I have endeavored to describe, namely, a direct, earnest, familiar address of a man speaking to men, in language which they understand, upon a single important truth which it is of the highest interest for him to make plain, and for them to retain.

## CHAPTER V.

### GESTURE.

NO more certain sign of the presence of oratorical power can be given, than freedom and propriety of gesture. The system of Delsarte is based upon this fact, and he has simply formulated his rules, in accordance with his observation of the natural expression of thought and emotion, in great orators, actors, and singers. The orator, in the exaltation of delivery, is a living proof of the theological doctrine that the soul is the form of the body. Heavy, awkward, inert in an ordinary mood of tranquillity, he becomes transfigured in the pulpit, or on the rostrum. Intellect, emotion, passion, all reveal themselves in what Cicero calls the language of the body.

The power of expressive gesture is innate, or most intimately associated with a peculiarly sensitive and emotional temperament. Gesture, in this sense, cannot be taught. It is spontaneous.

Happily, the preacher is not expected to excel in this power. Indeed, the gravity of his office forbids any violent or merely mimetic gesture. If, however, he is a true orator, he is a law to himself, and what in others seems exaggerated or dramatic is felt to be appropriate.

A dignified and manly attitude secures attention and respect by its indication of self-command, and conscious power and authority to teach. Here, good taste and sense are your best guides. The quieter and more composed you are, at the beginning of the sermon, the quieter will the congregation become. Wait until every noise in the church is stilled. If you begin speaking before the congregation have settled themselves in the pews, the noise will continue. Stop and wait, and all will become quiet.

Gymnastic exercises will give you ease and flexibility of movement, which are the basis of all correct gesture. If you cannot make any gesture at all, console yourself with Ruskin's opinion, that the orator should make no gesture, as it diverts the mind from the calm reception of truth.

To insure a certain grace and effectiveness of manner, have a judicious friend to point out to you any awkwardness he may observe, or any unseemly gesture or grimace, into which we all unconsciously fall, if left to ourselves. As you never know your own fault in this respect, it is needless here to enumerate.

The exterior being the index of the internal sentiment, you must begin to learn gesture from within. Perfect self-possession dominates an audience. They feel that you are master of the situation. This self-possession, which is also the mark of a gentleman, can come only from your knowledge of the sermon. If you have memorized it imperfectly, your strained expression of countenance, and the vacant eye will tell the tale. You are reciting a piece.

If you really and truly feel the sentiment, your gestures will be correct, no matter how widely they deviate from the fashion-plates in books of elocution. Your own personality, your individuality, then speaks, and you reveal yourself. The soul leaps to your eyes, raises the hand, advances the foot. Surrender yourself to the inspiration. You cannot go far wrong. The mischievous teaching of a set of conventional gestures only represses the native ardor of the soul. Training, suggestion, will come to you later. Your gesture is your own. It may be too vehement; it may be awkward. Be of good courage. These are only defects, not faults.

Gesture is a sign of emotion. If you do not feel, do not gesticulate.

As no one but a great orator can make gesture speak, never attempt the grand style, unless you are certain that you are an orator.

But as you are, or certainly will become, a good speaker, study the natural expression of the hand, in laying down the law, in pointing out a course of action, in invitation, in repelling. You can learn this, by simply watching the unaffected movements of those around you.

Cardinal Manning had only one gesture, that of the index finger. But do not use it because he did.

Plant yourself firmly on your feet. This gives an air of solidity and self-possession. Do not walk up and down the altar.

Speak straight before you, if you are in a large church, or in one with many pillars. Bobbing the head from one side to the other diverts the current of sound, which follows an invariable law, like a wave on a lake.

A certain dignity and majesty of manner dispenses with gesture. We can do much to supply the place of gesture, by impressive looks and tones.

Keep your self-control. If you lose the thread of your discourse, do not betray that you are in a quandary. Speak on. Say the Te Deum in English, or anything devotional that you remember. Here, your knowledge of the rhetorical pause will serve you in good stead.

If you are of opinion that you can learn gesture, go to an intelligent friend, and let him watch your movements in declamation. Be entirely unreserved. With no other guide than his eye, he will be able to tell you, whether you are likely to learn or not. Remember that very little gesticulation will answer all the requirements of an ordinary discourse.

There is one accomplishment in the power of us all to perfect, which is really more fascinating than the most studied gesture. It is the air and manner of a gentleman. This shows itself quite as plainly on the altar, as in the drawing-room. That indefinable air of good breeding, which distinguishes a gentleman, and which cannot be assumed and laid aside, but accompanies him everywhere, for it is a part of himself, will lend its charm to your manner in the pulpit, and make up for your want of grand gestures. We cannot all be orators, but the cultivation of humane feelings, courtesy to all, the poor especially, high and noble thinking, holiness of life, due observance of the usages of good society, will stamp their charming traces upon our action and speech in the pulpit, and produce effects which the most perfect declamation, without them, will seek after in vain.

The best book for the attainment of the

proper manner of the pulpit, is the ceremonial. If we know our ceremonies well, we shall never act awkwardly in the sanctuary. Going into the pulpit and leaving it, should be marked with proper slowness and dignity.

Delsarte says, that the reverent signing of the cross before the sermon, at once places the priest in command of his audience. We have so many positive aids toward making our preaching effective, that we need not deplore our inability to make gestures. The robed figure, the stole of authority, the calm, impressive attitude of the ambassador of the Most High, would seem to render all gesture superfluous.

# CHAPTER VI.

## THE PUBLIC READING OF ENGLISH DEVOTIONS.

IT is clear from the admitted difficulty of reading properly the English Book of Common Prayer, in the public service of the Church of England, that some attention is due to our own reading of occasional English prayers in public. There are now so many devotions conducted in the vernacular, so many confraternities and sodalities that hold public service in English, that we must recognize the necessity of careful preparation for such ministrations.

It is hard to convince an educated man that he does not know how to read aloud his own language. He does not blunder in pronunciation; he observes every comma; he has a loud voice; yet he reads badly.

Dogberry held that reading and writing come by nature, and there is truth in the idea, at least as regards expressiveness in reading. This is largely the gift of nature, the result of good vocal organs, under the control of a fine, emotional temperament. But good reading of any kind is rare. The reading of public prayer is peculiarly difficult, and none but a very thoughtless man will attempt to read the Scriptures, or indeed, any book of devotion, aloud in church, until he has made some preparation, or given frequent thought and practice to the laws of vocal delivery. Consider how difficult a language we have to articulate. Byron humorously contrasts the English "guttural splutter-all" with the melody of the Italian. The genius of the English tongue sacrifices harmony to strength. Cardinal Wiseman says that no language needs the help of gesture more than the English, and no people use it less. A German sounds nearly every letter of his polysyllabic words; an Italian rolls out every vowel, even in his so-called diphthongs. In France, public reading is classed with the fine arts. We expect a man to understand us from a grunt, half a verb, and, if we are very explicit, a nod of the head. If, with all our care in addressing the people from the pulpit, we often fail to make ourselves understood, how much more difficult it is to read prayers, with our back to the congregation, as when we face the altar?

In the public reading of prayers, we must depend entirely upon the management of the voice. Good taste and approved custom require us to use the monotone, which carries well, if carefully articulated.

An acoustic law requires us to read very slowly, if we read, facing the altar. The sounds strike the irregular surface in front of us, and they rebound with difficulty.

When an actor has to speak, with his

back to the audience, he pauses after nearly every word, and makes very few inflections.

Run your eye over the next line of the prayer, and speak it, holding your head erect. If you bury your face in the book, even the altar boys will misplace the amens.

We must beware of preaching in our prayer, if we would escape the censure incurred by the minister, who, under pretence of addressing Heaven, poured hot shot into the delinquent pew-holders.

Every prayer has a central thought. Try to bring this out, simply, sincerely, unaffectedly. Let it be your reverent study to pronounce aright the sacred name of Jesus.

The private preparation of our public reading should consist in a careful perusal of the matter aloud. Rarely attempt to read in public a prayer off-hand. If the people are not familiar from custom with the subject of the devotion, read the title of the prayer, in a clear, loud, measured tone, and pause for a moment, before beginning the body of the prayer.

The Sunday announcements afford us another practice in public reading. Indistinctness in these, sometimes gives rise to ludicrous misunderstandings, as in the case of the man who thought that a Lenten regulation read: "Custom has made it lawful, to take, in the morning, some warm *liquor*."

The impressive reading of the Gospel bespeaks attention for your sermon. Indeed, nothing awakens deeper attention than the proper reading of the word of God. The people never tire of that Beauty, ever ancient, ever new. They know the Sunday Gospels by heart, yet they listen with ever fresh attention.

We have a proper horror of a camp-meeting tone, yet solemnity must be the prevailing key. Be simple, and observe the natural modulations. Pause before and after the emphatic word. What that word is, you must study out for yourself. No two men ever read alike the same passage, or ever will. Cast-iron rules for emphasis, time, force, etc., are positively pernicious. Use your judgment, taste, feeling. The very attempt you make, will help to develop them.

In reading encyclicals, episcopal letters, and similar documents, study variety of tone. Cicero characterizes the judgment of the ear as *superbissimum*. We demand a discord in music, a rough line in poetry, for a change. You will save your reading from monotony, by changing now and then the key or the time. The same general direction applies to delivery. Change, change! If every style of writing is good, except the tedious, every style of speaking is good, except the monotonous.

## CHAPTER VII.

### DAILY HELPS TO IMPROVEMENT.

SENATOR ROSCOE CONKLING was asked how he acquired the faultless pronunciation, and the grammatical accuracy which marked even his impromptu addresses. "By attending to them in my private conversation," he answered.

We cannot neglect the ordinary laws of good English, in our daily chats, without showing the effects in the pulpit. Slovenly pronunciation, indifferent grammar, the habitual use of slang, a habit of slurring or dropping syllables will go with us into the pulpit.

The basis of public speech being conversation, we must give heed to our manner of daily talk. A little care and attention will enable us to frame complete sentences, instead of the half phrases and ejaculations, into which indolence tempts us. The freedom of conversation need not let the subject go hunting for a verb, and meet the wrong one. Conversation, which, in the old world is studied as a delightful art, threatens to become a lost one with us. Society, in general, has no resource but cards.

Still, we are a nation of talkers, and we need not go far, to find grand masters in the art. Become interested in an important and interesting subject, and discuss it with an intelligent friend. Visit the literary society connected with your church, and do not disdain to take part in those debates which, no doubt, are destined to shake the world. An hour in the school will brighten you up, more than you may care to acknowledge.

Remember that you are, by profession, a public speaker. People will look up to you as an authority. The church is filled with young folk, fresh from the grammar and the dictionary. Not even Cæsar is above grammar. Half-educated persons are the sharpest critics. They make no allowance for a slip in syntax, or a false pronunciation. When you are in doubt about the spelling, the pronunciation, or above all, the meaning of a word, consult the dictionary.

To acquire a command of simple and vigorous English, I recommend you to read the authors of the last century. Addison, Swift, Edmund Burke, and Goldsmith write for the understanding of plain men. You know from all the teachers of rhetoric, that inflated diction and sesquipedalian words offend against the highest canons of good taste. It is said of Molière, that he used to read his plays to his washerwoman, and any word that she could not understand, he would strike out.

Our education having been conducted so extensively in Latin, that language inevitably affects our English style. We must be on the alert with the army of Latin words which we have, it is true, under our command, but which may easily become our Prætorian Guard. Most of our older Catholic English literature, very good for matter, is disfigured by Latinisms and Gallicisms, from the circumstance that the authors were obliged to get their education on the Continent, owing to the proscriptive laws against Catholics in England. They lost the grace and flexibility of the English idiom.

Enrich your mind with some of the great passages of Shakespeare and Milton. The best of any language is in its poetry.

I question the utility of much reading of sermons. Better your own thoughts, in your own words, however far they fall below the magnificence of a great writer's.

You are to speak simple truth, not read or recite a finished essay. Your own words, warm from the heart, are, for effect, worth a library of sermons not your own. Only in so far as you can assimilate the thought of a writer, is he of benefit to you.

Thinking, meditation, reflection are the fountains of eloquence. If you had no book but the New Testament, that, with reflection, would furnish matter for a lifetime of preaching.

Read little and slowly, frequently pausing to take in the full meaning of the author. Never read what you cannot relish. It is a waste of time. The mind retains only that in which it delights. Once study becomes a task, it is fruitless.

The end of all education is to give a certain pliancy and quickness to the mind. Do not mistake the means for the end.

Waste no time in regretting that you have forgotten much of your college learning, your Greek and Hebrew. All these studies did the only work which is of permanent value. They developed and trained your intelligence, and it is partly what it is, because of them. But now that your mind is quick, vigorous, able to grasp ideas, and estimate their value, apply it to worthy thought. Muse on the eternal truths, the lessons of the Gospel, the commandments of God, the subjects which bear upon your own salvation, and that of your people. These are themes worthy of the contemplation of angels. They elevate and ennoble the intellect. Try to master them by your own living thought, under the guidance of Divine Faith.

If you exert your powers, trained by study and experience, you cannot fail to preach well. Too many books will only confuse and benumb you. If you candidly acknowledge the truth, you will say that you never obtained exactly what you wanted from any sermon-book. The works that helped you were those that made you think, such as commentaries, sketches of sermons, books of spiritual reading, etc.

To keep in touch with the times, take one good journal, and one good Review. Much reading of newspapers vitiates any style you may have, and, as you never dream of trying to remember what you read in them, they are practically useless, as means of mental cultivation.

You may inquire, with perfect propriety, of a sensible friend, what part or parts of your discourse make a good impression. Find out wherein lies your talent or power, and cultivate that. This is all our Lord will demand.

There is the highest authority for the declaration, that our salvation is intimately connected with our faithful ministry of the Divine Word. This thought is one full of awe and inspiration.

Do not lay aside this little book, without a resolve to give some of its hints a trial. The end of thought is action. You are hopeless, if you think that you are perfect.

Take up for exercise at least one of the points. If preaching leaves you hoarse and exhausted, begin the natural manner of delivering your sermon as a talk. If you cannot make your words carry, give your attention to articulation. If you never think of declaiming on a week-day, now begin. Do a little, at least on Saturday. All I ask is that you give these principles a fair trial.

"No day without a line" was the maxim and practice which led Appelles to immortality. The voice of octogenarian Gladstone thrills the House of Commons like a trumpet. The acting and tones of Henry Irving in "Becket," send his hearers weeping to their homes. These men labor for an earthly crown. They put us to the blush.

We are invested with the mission of the Apostles. Let us strive to render ourselves worthy of the sublimest of embassies—"Christ speaking by us." Since creation, God carries out His purposes by secondary causes, and with fit instruments. Let us be ready when the Master calls us to proclaim His message; to be for Him, the Voice in the wilderness, the Trumpet in Sion, the herald of the Great King.

www.ingramcontent.com/pod-product-compliance
Lightning Source LLC
Chambersburg PA
CBHW020245090426
42735CB00010B/1844